KU-301-355

God's Friends

A Pointing Out Book

Text by Sylvia Mandeville
Illustrations by Richard Deverell

Scripture Union

47 Marylebone Lane, London W1M 6AX

First published 1977 by
Scripture Union
47 Marylebone Lane,
London W1M 6AX

© Scripture Union.
All rights reserved.
No part of this publication may be
reproduced, stored in a retrieval
system, or transmitted in any form
or by any means, electronic,
mechanical, photocopying,
recopying or otherwise, without the
prior permission of
Scripture Union.

ISBN 0 85421 523 9

Designed by Tony Cantale
Research by Christine Deverell
Printed in Great Britain by
Purnell & Sons Ltd., Paulton, Bristol

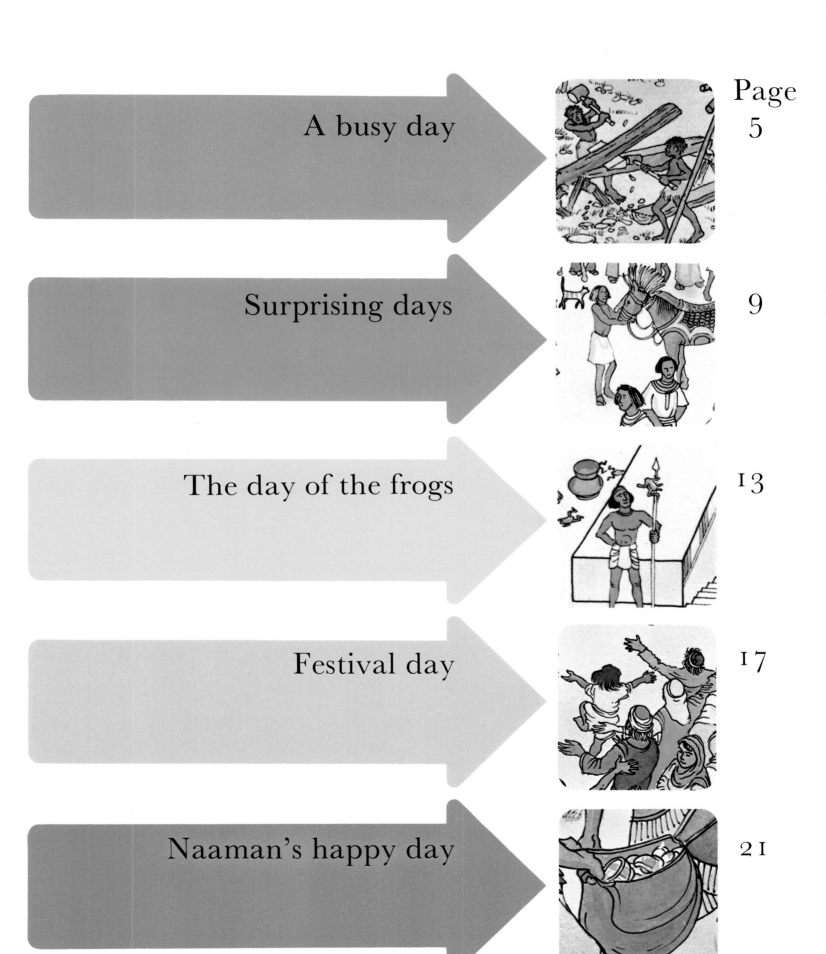

A busy day — Page 5

Surprising days — 9

The day of the frogs — 13

Festival day — 17

Naaman's happy day — 21

Exploring the Bible

To boys and girls:
Here is a book for you, with

- stories to read
- pictures to look at
- things to do

The book tells you a lot about some of God's friends who lived long before Jesus was born.

On the 'things to do' pages you will find puzzles, questions, and ideas for making things, as well as suggestions for writing and drawing.

If you get a scrap book you can stick your stories and pictures into it, and so make your own 'God's friends' book.

To parents and teachers:
Boys and girls, together with parents, friends and teachers, will gain immense pleasure from exploring the five stories which comprise this book.

The Pointing Out series is, however, designed to provide not only pleasure; it is a teaching aid— for home and church and school. All the books are based on a threefold principle: listen, look and do—each activity complementing the others.

Our aim is not only to bring home through the use of vivid detail the content and teaching of the Bible stories, but also to help boys and girls to see and absorb the background against which the events took place.

As well as listening to the stories, girls and boys will love to study the two-page picture spreads, discovering a host of detail which adds interest and depth to the incidents depicted.

Both the stories and the pictures are reinforced by the material on the activity pages which sends the reader back to the pictures again and again.

As the children are involved in these activities the message of God's Word will come across in terms which are relevant to their age and experience.

Bible verses are from the Good News Bible
© American Bible Society.

Titles in this series:
Meet Jesus
God's friends

A busy day

Hammer, bang, crash! Hammer, bang, crash! Noah and his family had started another day's hard work.

After months of chopping down trees and cutting them into planks, they were now building the ark, and it was at last beginning to look like a big boat. Noah was very careful how he built it. 'We must make it exactly as God told me,' he said.

'Will we get it finished in time, before the flood comes?' one of his sons asked.

Noah paused to think. 'If God was careful enough to warn me that a great flood was coming and tell me how to build the ark, then you can be sure he has given us enough time to make it. But that doesn't mean wasting time! Help me with this plank.'

'*If* the flood ever comes!' said a man standing nearby. 'You'll look stupid if you're left with this great boat stuck here by a tiny stream.'

'Yes, and with all these animals penned up,' laughed a woman.

'Be quite sure,' Noah said sternly, 'the flood will come. Change your lives. Stop your angry quarrels and murders, your fighting and your wicked thoughts. Live how God wants. Join us in the work, and be safe inside the ark when the flood comes.'

'What, with all those wild animals? No, thank you!' jeered the man. Just then an angry roaring was heard. 'The lions again,' said Noah's wife. 'They're always hungry. What a lot of work they make!'

'It's the snakes I don't like,' said the wife of one of Noah's sons. 'Must we really take them, too?'

'Snakes as well, that's what God said,' Noah answered, as he started work again.

At last it was all finished. Then God told Noah to go into the big houseboat with his family and all the animals. After seven days God did what he had said. The rain fell, and there was a great flood. But God looked after the people and the animals in the ark, and kept them safe. (*You can read this story in Genesis 6.9 to 7.24.*)

A busy day

Some things to do:

Noah

Find this man on the big picture. His name is Noah.
● Copy these sentences into your notebook, and write in the missing words.

Noah was a . . . man. Noah . . . God. Noah had three sons called . . . , . . . and . . . Noah was in charge of . . . the houseboat.

The missing words
loved   Shem   good   Ham
Japheth   building
● Read Genesis 6.9-14, and check your answers.

The houseboat

God told Noah to build a houseboat. He told him exactly what to do.
● Copy these letters into your notebook but leave out the letter X. You will then find out what Noah did.

NXOAXHXXDIXDXXEVXERY
XTXHXINXGXXTHXATXX
GOXDXXCOXMXMANXDXED

God's instructions to Noah are in

● Read the verses and answer these questions about the houseboat.
How long was the houseboat?
How wide and how high was it?
How many decks had it?
From what was it made?

With what was it covered both inside and out? Where was the door?

Make a houseboat

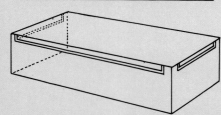

You need a long, shallow box, strips of wood or thick cardboard, glue, scissors and black paint.
1. Cut the front off your box so that you can see inside it.
2. Cut a slit around the top of the box as shown but do not cut the corners of the box.
3. Cut out three cardboard decks. These should be slightly smaller than the top of your box.
4. Glue strips of wood or thick card inside the box where you want the decks to be. Make sure they are level.

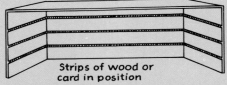

Strips of wood or
card in position

5. When the glue is dry slide the decks into position.

The animals and birds

Make a list of the animals and birds in the picture. Look in a book to find out the names of the animals you don't recognize. Why did Noah want the animals collected together (Genesis 6.19-20)?

The people working

Look again at the large picture. Make a list of the different jobs the people are doing. Draw some of their tools.
● Look at the ladies by the food. What are they doing? What did God tell them to do in Genesis 6.21?

The people laughing

These people are laughing at Noah. What do you think they are saying?
Only Noah loved God and believed that he would send a flood. Noah continued to build the houseboat when other people laughed at him and thought he was silly.

Kept safe

When the houseboat was finished, Noah, his family, the animals and the birds went inside. There was a great flood, just as God had said, and everything was covered with water. But God kept everybody in the houseboat safe.

Over one year later the flood had gone. It was safe for Noah, his family and the creatures to leave the houseboat (Genesis 8.13-19).

Everybody was happy and thanked God for keeping them safe.
● Draw a picture of Noah, his wife, their three sons and their wives when they left the houseboat.
● Try to think of a time when you have been kept safe and make up a prayer to thank God for it.

Surprising days

Year after year there was no rain. The land was dry and brown. No corn or fruit grew. Everyone was hungry—except the people in Egypt. They had plenty of corn, stored up in great tall buildings. Many years before, when there were good harvests, God had told Prime Minister Joseph to save the corn. Now all the people came to buy this corn from Joseph.

Joseph was busy, but not happy. Every day he stared at the people who came to him, and every day he was disappointed and sad. His servants noticed it.

'It's as if he's on the look-out for someone,' his chief servant whispered one day. 'He's been like this for months now. Ever since that family of brothers came from Canaan to buy corn.'

'Yes,' said another servant. 'He told them to come back with their youngest brother.'

Just then, the servants heard Joseph calling them. They hurried to him, and there, bowing low before Joseph, they saw the family they had been talking about. Joseph was excited. 'Take these men to my palace,' he ordered. 'And prepare a feast.'

When Joseph returned from work, the feast began. He felt very happy and very sad at the same time. This was because he knew a secret, which the men did not know. *He was their long lost brother*. Years before they had sold him as a slave. They thought he must be dead. But God had cared for him and now he was Prime Minister of Egypt.

Joseph could not decide whether or not to tell the brothers who he was. 'I know,' he said to himself. 'I will give them a test to see if they have changed, and can be trusted.'

The next day Joseph found out that his brothers were now good and loving. Then he could not keep his secret any longer. 'I am Joseph,' he said. 'Don't be upset and frightened. You were cruel to me, but God has made it turn out for everyone's good.'

When the brothers saw that Joseph had forgiven them, they cried and laughed and talked for a long time. They were very happy. After that all Joseph's family and his old father came to live with him in Egypt, and God looked after them all.

(You can read about this in Genesis 41.37-57 and in chapters 42-45.)

Surprising days

Some things to do:

The Prime Minister

Joseph was the Prime Minister of all Egypt. The king made Joseph the Prime Minister. Sort out the jumbled letters to find out what he said to Joseph.

'I will TUP you in charge of my YRTNUOC and all my people will YEBO your orders.' (Genesis 41.40)

● Why was Joseph made the Prime Minister? This code will help you to find out.

1	2	3	4	5	6	7	8	9	10	11	12	13
a	b	c	d	e	f	g	h	i	j	k	l	m

14	15	16	17	18	19	20	21	22	23
n	o	p	q	r	s	t	u	v	w

24	25	26
x	y	z

1. The 11, 9, 14, 7 had two 4, 18, 5, 1, 13, 19 which troubled him.

2. God 8, 5, 12, 16, 5, 4 Joseph to 21, 14, 4, 5, 18, 19, 20, 1, 14, 4 the dreams.

3. For 19, 5, 22, 5, 14, 25, 5, 1, 18, 19 there would be plenty of 6, 15, 15, 4.

4. After that no 3, 18, 15, 16, 19 would 7, 18, 15, 23 for seven years.

5. People would be 8, 21, 14, 7, 18, 25.

6. During the seven 7, 15, 15, 4, 25, 5, 1, 18, 19 they needed to 19, 1, 22, 5,   6, 15, 15, 4.

7. During the seven 2, 1, 4 years they needed to 19, 8, 1, 18, 5 the 6, 15, 15, 4 they had 19, 20, 15, 18, 5, 4.

8. They needed 19, 15, 13, 5, 2, 15, 4, 25 to be in 3, 8, 1, 18, 7, 5 of the food.

9. The king chose 10, 15, 19, 5, 16, 8 to be this 13, 1, 14.

10. This was God's 16, 12, 1, 14 for Joseph.

God was with Joseph all the time and cared for him.

Storing the corn

These are the tall granaries in which Joseph stored the corn.

Look at the granaries on the big picture. How were they filled with corn?

The corn was used to make bread.

The brothers

Lots of people came to Joseph for food. Among them were Joseph's brothers. What are they doing in the picture below?

They did not recognize Joseph because he looked different. His hair was a different style. He had no beard. He wore Egyptian clothes.

The quarrel

When Joseph was a boy he and his brothers quarrelled. Genesis chapter 37 describes their quarrel.

● What do verses 2, 3 and 5-7 tell us about Joseph when he was young?
● What do verses 4, 8 and 11 tell us about his brothers?
● What did Joseph's brothers do (verses 27, 28)?
● What did they tell their father (verses 31-33)?

The tests

Find the servants in the picture. What are they thinking?

When Joseph met his brothers he wondered what to do. Should he tell them who he was?
● What did Joseph tell them the first time they came for food (Genesis 42.19, 20)?

The second time they came Joseph gave the brothers another test, so that he would know whether they had changed and whether they were honest and told the truth.
● You can read about this test in Genesis chapter 44.

After the test Joseph told his brothers who he was. They were sorry for what they had done to him and he forgave them.

Make a model

Cut 2 holes in 2 sides of a box

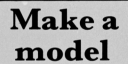

Cut out 'screen'

Turn rods to move pictures

Place wooden rods through holes

Attach picture roll to rods

You need a long piece of paper which is as wide as your television model. Draw a series of pictures to show on your television.

Your pictures should illustrate these verses from Genesis:

1. 37.3	**2.** 37.18-24
3. 37.27, 28	**4.** 42.5-8
5. 42.35	**6.** 45.14, 15

Copy these words at the end of your paper to form the last picture.
But the Lord was with Joseph and blessed him.

Attach your pictures to the television set. Show the story of Joseph to your friends.

The day of the frogs

It had been fun to begin with. The children had enjoyed it—waking to find bright green frogs leaping over their beds! But mothers trying to cook found frogs in their baking pans. Farmers milking cows found frogs falling into their buckets. As the day passed the frogs increased. It was impossible to work, to sleep or to play. It was fun no longer.

The mighty Pharaoh in his palace was angry. However fast his slaves swept the frogs away, some would jump back just as he put his foot to the ground. They were even on his throne. It had to stop! Pharaoh was angry—yet it was all his fault.

Moses and Aaron had come to him, asking that the Israelites be set free from slavery to go into the desert to worship God. Pharaoh had refused. The Jews were his slaves. They were his brick makers and builders. He would not let them go.

And now this punishment had come: these frogs, causing chaos everywhere.

Pharaoh decided to send for Moses. He would give in. He would let the people go—anything to get rid of the slimy frogs.

Moses and Aaron arrived. They stood calmly before Pharaoh. They were old men who were brave and strong. Their simple clothes were out of place in the glittering surroundings of the palace.

Pharaoh sat on the throne. It was difficult to look important and dignified with frogs leaping over his lap and peering round his ears! 'Pray to your God to take these frogs away,' he said sternly to Moses. 'Then, when they have gone, I will let your people go to worship God.'

'Tell me when you want me to pray,' said Moses, 'and at that time the frogs will leave your houses.'

'Pray tomorrow,' Pharaoh answered.

'I will pray for the frogs to go,' said Moses. 'Then you will know that there is no other God like the Lord our God and we must obey him.' Quietly Moses and Aaron left the royal palace.

The next day, when Moses prayed to God, all the frogs died.

(You can read this story in Exodus 8.1-14)

The day of the frogs

Some things to do:

The frogs

Find these people on the picture. What are they doing? What do they think about the frogs?
● Find out all you can about frogs. Use a book from the library to help you.
● Draw pictures of frogs' spawn, tadpoles, froglets and frogs.

Find this man, the cat and two frogs on the picture. Think about what they are doing.

Give them all names and make up a funny story about them.
● Unjumble these sentences. They will help you to find out why there are so many frogs. Each sentence begins with Pharaoh's name.

Pharaoh the king Egypt of was new.

Pharaoh Joseph remember not did.

Pharaoh Israelites his slaves made the.

Pharaoh young the boys killed.

Pharaoh whipped had people.

Pharaoh love God not did.

Pharaoh not would the Israelites let go.

Pharaoh not would listen God's to warning.

Pharaoh

Find Pharaoh, the king, on the picture. Why is he so angry?

This code will help you to work out God's warning message to Pharaoh.

A	B	C	D	E	F	G	H	I
○	△	▽	□	●	▲	▼	■	◉

J	K	L	M	N	O	P	Q	R
◮	⧨	⊡	⊟	⊖	⬖	▽	⊟	∅	◭

S	T	U	V	W	X	Y	Z
▽	◪	◐	◭	▲	▽	◧	⊗	◭

● Read Exodus chapter 8, verses 3 and 4. They will tell you the rest of God's message.

Pharaoh refused to let the Israelites go. He disobeyed God, so he deserved to be punished. It was Pharaoh's fault that God sent the plague of frogs to punish him.

Moses

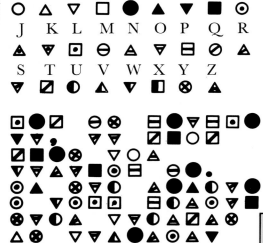

This is Moses and his brother Aaron. Moses is standing on the left. God chose Moses to be the leader of his people, the Israelites.

Find Moses on the big picture. Where is he standing? To whom is he speaking? How would you feel if you had to speak to a king who was wicked, cruel and angry?

● What did Pharaoh say to Moses? Use the code to find out.

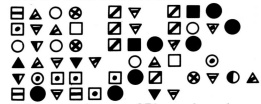

● Draw a picture of Pharaoh and write what he said in a speech balloon beside him.
● What did Moses reply (Exodus 8.9)?
● Draw a picture of Moses and write his reply in a speech balloon.

When he told Pharaoh that God would answer the prayer Moses said something important.

This sentence has been written backwards. What does it say?

.doG ruo ,drol eht ekil doG rehto on si ereht taht wonk lliw uoY.

Make a scroll

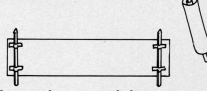

You need a long sheet of paper, crayons or felt pens, two long pencils or knitting needles, ribbon and some sticky tape. Write Moses' message on your paper. Decorate around the edges. Tape the pencils into position. Roll up your scroll. Tie a ribbon round it.

Remember to read the message regularly.

God answers prayer

What did Pharaoh do when all the frogs were dead (Exodus 8.15)? God showed Pharaoh ten times that he is the only God. Nine times Pharaoh was stubborn and would not let the Israelites go. The tenth time he set them free. Then the Israelites left Egypt. Moses led them away to worship God in the desert.

Festival day

King David was happy. The priests were happy. The people were happy. They were all singing and praising God because at last King David was bringing God's covenant box into Jerusalem, his new capital city.

With no shoes on, and stripped to the waist, King David was leaping and dancing. Behind him marched a great procession. First came the priests, carrying the covenant box very carefully on poles on their shoulders. Then specially chosen singers danced past, singing loudly to God. And musicians came, playing their instruments—cymbals, harps and lyres, trumpets, horns and tambourines. All the noises resounded and rang through Jerusalem.

And all around, from the tree tops, leaning over walls, peeping over parapets and through windows, the men, women and children of Israel sang and cheered as the procession went by. They stared at the covenant box.

'Look, there it is!'

'Isn't it marvellous!' they whispered to each other. 'Look at the gold and the carvings. Look at the winged cherubim.'

'That box is hundreds of years old,' said one man. 'It's more important than anything else. Moses made it. And inside are the two slabs of stone with God's ten commandments on them.'

Slowly the priests walked through the city carrying the precious box to the Tent which King David had put up for it. Gently they lowered it on to a table.

Then what a noise the happy people made! What clamour and clashing there was, what singing and dancing! Everyone crowded all round the Tent, for a service of thanksgiving to God. King David announced a new hymn written specially for this occasion. Standing round the covenant box the singers sang the hymn triumphantly, and the people shouted 'Amen'.

King David gave food to all the people —a loaf of bread, a piece of roasted meat and some raisins. And after that it was late. Everyone felt tired and peaceful, and it was time to go home.

*(You can read this story in
1 Chronicles 15.25-29; 16.1-3)*

Some things to do:

The children

Find these children on the picture. What are they running to see? Pretend that you are with them and that you are a television reporter. Write or tape-record a report of what you can see and hear.

The covenant box

King David and the people were happy. Follow the arrows to find out why they were happy.

```
T  Y→W E→T I→N O→D
↓  ↑  ↓  ↑  ↓  ↑  ↓  ↓
H→E E→R A→K G→G S
O→V A→N B T→O R→U L→E
↓  ↑  ↑  ↗  ↓  ↑  ↓  ↑  ↓
C  E→N T O→X J→E S→A M
```

Find the covenant box on the picture. It was important to King David and the people.

● Now get your Bible and turn to Exodus chapter 25. Read verses 10 to 22 to find out what God told Moses to do. What did God tell Moses to put inside the box (verse 16)?

Thanking God

King David and his people were glad that they could take God's covenant box into Jerusalem. What did they do to show that they were happy?

Unjumble the words for the answer.
They **decnad** and **gnas.**
They **deyalp stnemurtsni.**

● Draw some pictures to show what King David and his people did. Underneath your picture write: *King David and his people did these things to thank God and show him that they were happy.*

Instruments for saying thank you

Look at the different instruments which the people are playing.
● Find out what they are called.

Make some instruments

Drum

Decorate a tin. Use coloured paper or gloss paint for this. Stretch thick plastic over the top of the tin so that it is tight. Use a strong elastic band to hold the plastic in place.

Shaker

Place some dried peas, rice or small stones inside a plastic container. Replace the lid. Paste small pieces of newspaper over the shaker. When the glue is dry, paint the shaker and varnish it.

Music and dancing

Use your instruments to make up tunes or rhythms. While you are playing your music think about some things which make you happy and thank God for them.

● Find this boy. Find some more people who are thanking God by dancing.
● Think of somebody for whom you want to thank God, and make up a thank you dance.

A new song

Psalm 96 is part of King David's special thank you song. Find it in your Bible.
● Design a book-mark or poster with the words of verse 2 written on it or write your own song on it.

Naaman's happy day

At the first sound of chariot wheels Elisha rushed from his house. He had to see the face of Naaman, the foreign man who was leaping down from the chariot.

That morning Naaman had come to Elisha, asking to be healed. His face and body had been covered in ugly sores and white patches. Elisha told Naaman to go and wash in the River Jordan. Now he was back again. Elisha was sure that God had healed him.

As soon as Naaman saw Elisha, he strode towards him. 'I did it. I did what you said,' Naaman called out. 'I bathed in the river seven times, and your God has healed me! Look at my face—and my arms—not a mark on them. Now I know that your God is the true God.'

Other people heard the noise and came running from their houses. They were amazed when they saw this foreign soldier praising their God.

'Look!' someone called out. 'Look what's happening now.'

From other chariots servants were jumping, carrying glittering and costly presents. Some held garments embroidered with jewels. Others had sacks of silver and gold. They spread out all these gifts for Elisha to see.

'These are for you,' Naaman said, 'to show my thanks.' But Elisha was not looking at the silver and gold, nor at the garments. He was looking at Naaman, and thanking God for curing him. Naaman's healing had been a gift from God. So how could Elisha receive silver and gold for it? 'As the Lord lives, whom I serve, I will not accept any presents,' he said. Naaman was puzzled and tried to persuade him, but Elisha would not give in. 'No presents, thank you,' he said firmly. He was about to turn away, when Naaman called out to him again. 'Could I have a load of earth to take back to Syria with me? From now on I will worship only your God, and I would like to do it on your soil.'

Elisha agreed, and Naaman's servants dug the earth. Then, praising God, Naaman returned rejoicing to his own country.

(You can read this story in 2 Kings 5.1-19)

Some things to do:

Elisha's friends

Look carefully at these people. They live near Elisha and they are Israelites. What are they wearing?

Now look for the Israelites on the big picture.
- How do they get their water?
- Where is the potter working?
- How do the ladies cook their meat?
- What are the houses like?
- What is the river like?
  Pretend that you live here. Write about your town, and the people who live in it.

Elisha

Unjumble these words to find out about Elisha. Every sentence begins with Elisha's name.

Israelite was Elisha an.
God Elisha loved.
Elisha called prophet was a.
always God obey wanted to Elisha.
helped people other Elisha.

Naaman

Find Naaman in the big picture. He is the man who is wet.

Unjumble these words. Every sentence begins with Naaman.

lived Naaman in Syria.
was rich Naaman.
an army was Naaman commander.
Naaman soldiers what told to do.
help Naaman needed.

God knows best

Think of your favourite game.
- Draw a picture of yourself playing the game. Underneath write a list of the rules of the game. What would happen if everyone decided to disobey the rules?
- Draw three road signs. What do they tell drivers to do? What would happen if the drivers took no notice of the signs?

It's best to OBEY the rules.
God gives RULES.

Elisha knew that it's best to OBEY God.

Learning to obey

Elisha D E P L E H Naaman. He sent a message to Naaman. The message told Naaman what God wanted him to do.

Hold this page to a mirror to find out what the message was. You can also read it in 2 Kings 5.10.

Go and wash seven times in the River Jordan.

Naaman was angry.
- What did he say (2 Kings 5.11, 12)?
- What happened (verses 13, 14)?
- How did Naaman feel (verse 15)?

Naaman learned that it's best to OBEY God.

The presents

Here is a Syrian. Find the other Syrians on the picture. What are they doing?
- Naaman wanted to give Elisha a present. What was it (2 Kings 5.5)?
- What did Elisha say to Naaman (2 Kings 5.16)?

Elisha did not want to accept a thank you present for something he had not done. Instead he wanted to thank God.

Make a garment

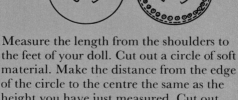

Make a garment for a doll or action man.

Measure the length from the shoulders to the feet of your doll. Cut out a circle of soft material. Make the distance from the edge of the circle to the centre the same as the height you have just measured. Cut out neck and sleeves as shown. Paste or sew beads, buttons, sequins or foil around the edges of the circle.